Healthy Kids Cookbook

These Healthy Dishes Can Help to Keep
Your Child Living a Healthy and Active
Life!

BY

Stephanie Sharp

License Notes

My deepest thanks for buying my book! Now that you have made this investment in time and money, you are now eligible for free e-books on a weekly basis! Once you subscribe by filling in the box below with your email address, you will start to receive free and discounted book offers for unique and informative books. There is nothing more to do! A reminder email will be sent to you a few days before the promotion expires so you will never have to worry about missing out on this amazing deal. Enter your email address below to get started. Thanks again for your purchase!

Just visit the link or scan QR-code to get started!

https://stephanie-sharp.subscribemenow.com

Table of Contents

Introduction

When looking into finding ways to help ensure that your child is getting enough nutrients, it is essential that you choose the right foods. We need to provide meals that will help power our children's growth and development. A way you can achieve this is to include the right kinds of foods in your child's daily diet. However, we all know this can be easier said than done. Many parents in today's world have hectic work schedules, making it very difficult for them to cook and prepare complete meals every day.

Living in this fast-paced world means that often kids are left to feed themselves, their food choices often being takeout or convenience foods which are often not good for their health. Making bad food choices can lead to serious health issues some of which can easily continue into adulthood such as diabetes.

To help promote good health in our children, it is vital that nutritional foods are included in their diets to encourage healthy development and growth. Some of the benefits of a healthy diet for children include:

- Better brain function
- Promotes normal development
- Strong Immune function
- Healthy Mental condition
- Keep Kids Alert and Active
- Helps Promote Healthy body weight

A great way to help prevent chronic diseases such as heart disease, obesity, high blood pressure, and type 2 diabetes is to have a healthy diet. If you instill now into your children how important eating healthy is, there is a higher chance that they will stick to including healthy food choices in their diet even in their adulthood.

Let us keep in mind that no child is a perfect feeder and including sugary foods once and a while in moderation is okay. As a responsible parent, you must make sure that the majority of the foods your child is eating are healthy and nutritious food choices. These healthy food choices will include foods such as:

- Meat and alternatives
- Milk and alternatives
- Grains
- Vegetables and Fruits

Try to monitor the amount and how often your child is eating sugary foods or convenience/take out foods. Remember that as a parent you play a central role in the promotion of your child's health. Consider the following list of things to help keep your child's health good:

Stipulate regular mealtimes and snacks, sharing meals with your child will help to encourage your child to eat healthy food choices.

Try to create meals that offer a balanced blend of foods groups mentioned above. Try to include at least two types of foods of the four food groups.

Teach your child to use utensils, a cup, etc. so that they can eat independently as soon as possible.

Feed your child homemade meals as often as possible try to avoid fast foods as much as possible.

Involve your child in grocery shopping. Teach your children how to read food labels, so they will understand what to look for and what the nutritional value is on the food they are choosing.

Note: Keep in mind that it is not unusual for a child's appetite to change from meal to meal. Also, feed them children-size portions, as they have small stomachs and can only eat as much as their body needs.

Chapter 1. Healthy Children's Breakfast Recipe Collection

1. Peanut Butter Banana Smoothie

This yummy recipe provides a nice balanced blend of nutrients from whole foodstuffs. This is a sweet smoothie for kids that includes bananas and honey. Peanut butter, on the other hand, offers proteins which help with tissue repair and bodybuilding.

Preparation Time: 5 minutes

Servings: 4

Ingredients:

- 2 cups milk
- 0.25 cup of all-natural peanut butter
- 4 bananas, medium
- 1 cup ice
- 1 teaspoon organic honey

Directions:

1. Mix all of your ingredients in a blender.
2. Blend the mixture until smooth.
3. Serve smoothie right away and enjoy!

Nutritional Information:

- Calories: 335
- Fat: 14g
- Carbs: 42g
- Fiber: 4g
- Protein: 14g
- Sugar: 27g

2. Chewy Pumpkin Bars

These pumpkin bars are super soft, chewy, and delicious, while they make a nutritious breakfast bar for kids. They will help to leave your child feeling full in the morning. You can prepare pumpkin bars ahead of time, and they are easy for children with only a few teeth to eat.

Preparation Time: 5 minutes

Total Cook Time: 20 minutes

Servings: 9

Ingredients:

- 0.25 cup chocolate chips (dark)
- 0.5 cup walnuts, chopped
- 1.5 tablespoons pumpkin pie spice
- 0.25 cup organic honey
- 1 cup canned pumpkin puree
- 2 cups oats, dry

Directions:

1. Preheat your oven to 350° Fahrenheit. Lightly grease your baking pan with a non-stick cooking spray.
2. In a mixing bowl add all of your ingredients and stir to combine.
3. Press your mixture into your baking dish.
4. Bake for ingredients for 20 minutes or until the top is firm and a golden color.
5. Allow cooling then slice into bite-size bars.
6. Serve warm and enjoy!

Note: You can store bars in an airtight container for up to 3 days.

Nutritional Information:

- Calories: 187
- Fat: 7g
- Carbs: 27g
- Fiber: 3g
- Protein: 4g
- Sugar: 12g

3. Sweet Potatoes Pancakes

This is a healthy recipe that your child will not get enough of. Filled with fiber, sweet potatoes will help promote a good and healthy digestive system. It will also help prevent gastric and duodenal ulcers.

Preparation Time: 10 minutes

Total Cook Time: 30 minutes

Servings: 4

Ingredients:

- 1 cup milk
- 1 cooked sweet potato, medium
- 1 egg
- 0.5 teaspoon cinnamon
- 0.5 teaspoon vanilla extract
- 0.25 teaspoon salt
- 2 teaspoons baking powder

Serve with:

- 4 teaspoons pure maple syrup
- 1 cup low-fat yogurt, vanilla
- 2 bananas (medium)

Directions:

1. Blend 0.5 cup mashed sweet potato, milk, egg, cinnamon, and vanilla into a blender until smooth.

2. Combine your baking powder, salt, and flour in a mixing-bowl, then add in the sweet potato mixture and mix until well combined.

3. If needed add in extra milk to reach the desired pancake batter.

4. In a large non-stick pan, lightly grease the pan with non-stick cooking spray. Add in the batter to the pan that is over medium-high heat on stove top.

5. Cook your pancakes for 5 minutes per side, or until the bubbles begin to form then flip them. Cook both sides of pancakes until they are browned.

6. Top the pancakes with some yogurt, sliced banana, and sprinkle a bit of maple syrup on top.

7. Serve the pancakes warm and enjoy!

Nutritional Information:

- Calories: 346
- Total Fat: 4g
- Carbs: 67g
- Fiber: 5g
- Protein: 11g
- Sugar: 32g

4. Fluffy Egg-less Pancakes

This pancake recipe is great for kids or people that have egg allergies. You can replace eggs with Ener-G egg replacer, chia or flax seeds, and banana puree for a healthy pancake recipe. You can top the pancakes with banana or strawberry slices to give the pancakes a real full fruit flavor to them.

Preparation Time: 5 minutes

Total Cook Time: 6 minutes per pancake

Servings: 4

Ingredients:

- 1 tablespoon vanilla extract
- 1.25 cups unsweetened almond milk
- 2 tablespoons coconut oil
- 1 tablespoon sugar
- 0.25 tablespoon salt
- 1 teaspoon baking powder
- 0.75 cup all-purpose flour
- 1 cup whole wheat flour
- Serve with:
- 2 cups vanilla yogurt (Greek)
- 4 medium nectarines (sliced)

Directions:

1. Mix the whole wheat flour, baking powder, salt, sugar, and all-purpose flour in a mixing bowl.

2. Add your coconut oil into another bowl along with, vanilla extract, and almond milk.

3. Mix your wet ingredients along with your dry ingredients, making sure to combine the mixture well.

4. In a large non-stick skillet spray it with cooking spray and place over medium heat on stove top.

5. Add about a quarter cup of mixture to the skillet and cook for three minutes per side. Flip the pancakes when they turn golden brown.

6. Repeat the process using the rest of the batter.

7. Top the pancakes with yogurt and serve with nectarine slices on top of yogurt or on the side and enjoy!

Nutritional Information:

- Calories: 421
- Total Fat: 10g
- Carbs: 72g
- Fiber: 5g
- Protein: 13g
- Sugar: 39g

5. Blueberry Pancakes

This is a yummy classic kid breakfast recipe. When blueberries become a little heated, they release a lot of flavor within your mouth. Your kids will be sure to be yearning for more of these pancakes in no time!

Preparation Time: 5 minutes

Total Cook Time: 6 minutes per pancake

Servings: 4

Ingredients:

- 1 teaspoon honey
- 1 cup milk
- 1 egg
- 1 teaspoon baking powder
- 0.5 cup whole wheat flour
- 1.5 cup graham cracker crumbs
- 0.5 cup blueberries
- Serve with:
- 1 cup blueberries
- 4 teaspoons pure maple syrup
- 4 teaspoons unsalted butter

Directions:

1. Mix the baking powder, flour, and graham cracker crumbs in a mixing bowl and set aside.
2. Whisk the egg, milk, and honey in a large bowl until well combined.
3. Mix the wet mixture and dry mixture and stir until well combined. Fold in the blueberries.
4. In a large non-stick skillet spray with non-stick cooking spray and place over medium heat on the stovetop.
5. Pancakes should be cooked 3 minutes per side, or until they are golden brown.
6. Repeat this process with remaining mixture.
7. Top pancakes with maple syrup, butter, and extra blueberries and enjoy!

Nutritional Information:

- Calories: 380
- Total Fat: 37g
- Carbs: 66g
- Fiber: 4g
- Protein: 8g
- Sugar: 31g

6. Banana Muffins

This recipe is light, fluffy, and moist, and is perfect muffins for kids. Make sure to use completely ripe bananas for the recipe (outside skin is black, and inside is brown), this will ensure a yummy banana flavor in the muffins.

Preparation Time: 10 minutes

Total Cook Time: 35 minutes

Servings: 18

Ingredients:

- 0.25 tablespoon salt
- 1.25 tablespoons baking powder
- 0.5 cup all-purpose flour
- 1.25 cup whole wheat flour
- 1 tablespoon cinnamon
- 2 tablespoons coconut oil
- 2 tablespoons vanilla extract
- 3 bananas, ripe
- 2 eggs
- 0.5 cup sugar
- 1 cup almond milk, unsweetened
- 0.5 tablespoons baking soda

Directions:

1. Preheat your oven to 400° Fahrenheit. Add a liner into each muffin tin (18 tins) and set aside.
2. Blend the sugar, eggs, bananas, vanilla, almond milk, and coconut oil in your blender until smooth.
3. In a mixing bowl, combine the wheat flour, all-purpose flour, baking soda, baking powder, salt, and cinnamon.
4. Combine the wet ingredients in a bowl, then add them to dry ingredients and mix well. Add the muffin mix to muffin tins, filling them about 0.75 full.
5. Now, bake your muffins for 35 minutes or until fully cooked. Serve muffins warm and enjoy!

Nutritional Information:

- Calories: 111
- Total Fat: 2g
- Carbs: 20g
- Fiber: 1g
- Protein: 2g
- Sugar: 9g

7. Breakfast Pizza

This is a great healthy recipe for kids as the carbohydrates found in naan bread are a good source of energy for kids. It also includes B vitamins which will help to keep your child's blood cells healthy. Berries are high in fiber and are good for your child's digestive system.

Preparation Time: 15 minutes

Total Cook Time: non-cook recipe

Servings: 4

Ingredients:

- 0.5 cup walnuts, chopped
- 1 cup blackberries
- 1 cup raspberries
- 4 large naan bread
- 1 teaspoon milk
- 1 teaspoon vanilla extract
- 0.25 cup honey
- 8-ounces, low-fat cream cheese

Directions:

1. Place honey, milk, vanilla, cream cheese, into a bowl and blend with a hand mixer until smooth.
2. Spread the mix on each piece of naan bread then top with walnuts and berries.
3. Serve and enjoy!

8. Apple Cinnamon Oatmeal Bar

These are tasty and easy to prepare oatmeal bars that are filled with nutrients for kids and are perfect for busy school mornings. Oatmeal bars are well-suited for the light breakfast eaters and can be served with a green smoothie for some veggie, or a boiled egg or a glass of milk.

Preparation Time: 15 minutes

Total Cook Time: 30 minutes

Servings: 8

Ingredients:

- 2.5 cups oats, dry
- 0.5 tablespoon baking powder
- 2 tablespoons cinnamon
- 0.25 tablespoons salt
- 0.5 cup coconut flakes
- 1 apple, diced
- 0.75 cup milk
- 0.5 cup honey
- 2 tablespoons vanilla extract
- 1 egg
- 0.75 cup applesauce (unsweetened)

Directions:

1. Start by preheating oven to 350° Fahrenheit, then grease your baking dish.
2. Blend a cup of oats in your blender then pour this mixture into a mixing bowl.
3. Add the remaining oats along with cinnamon, baking soda, and salt and combine.
4. In another mixing bowl, add the vanilla, egg, applesauce, milk, and honey. Stir this mixture into the dry ingredients until well combined.
5. Grate the apple then add the grated apple to the mix along with coconut flakes.
6. Fold into the mixture and add to baking dish. Bake for 30 minutes.
7. Allow to cool slightly, then cut the bars, serve and enjoy!

Nutritional Information:

- Calories: 243
- Total Fat: 5g
- Carbs: 45g
- Fiber: 4g
- Protein: 5g
- Sugar: 25g

Chapter 2. Healthy Children's Lunch Recipe Collection

9. Taco Bowl with Avocado Lime Dressing

This taco bowl recipe is an excellent dish for kids as well as the entire family. You can eat these with your kids while getting to try a variety of veggies and enjoying different kinds of tacos together.

Preparation Time: 8 minutes

Total Cook Time: 30 minutes

Servings: 4

Ingredients:

- 1 lime, sliced into wedges
- 1 avocado, chopped
- 0.5 tablespoon red onion, chopped
- 1 cup halved cherry tomatoes
- 2 cups water
- black pepper to taste
- sea salt to taste
- 6 cups Romaine lettuce, chopped
- 2 sweet potatoes, cut into cubes
- 0.5 cup corn, frozen
- 1 cup raw rice, brown

Dressing:

- 1 tablespoon garlic powder
- 2 tablespoons cilantro
- 1 avocado
- 0.33 cups water
- 2 tablespoons lime juice
- sea salt and black pepper to taste

Directions:

1. Preheat your oven to 400° Fahrenheit, allow the frozen corn to thaw.

2. On a baking sheet, line it with parchment paper, then place cubed sweet potatoes in a baking sheet.

3. Lightly, sprinkle your potatoes with salt and pepper and bake for 30 minutes at 400° Fahrenheit. During the cook time turn potatoes over once.

4. While the potatoes are baking, cook the rice-based upon the cooking directions on package. Use a fork to fluff the rice, then add in the corn and stir to combine.

5. Add the rice to a bowl, filling it about a quarter full of rice mixture. Add all the other ingredients, which will be chopped into small wedges.

6. In your blender combine your dressing ingredients and process until smooth. You decide to add a bit of water to thin it out.

7. Drizzle the dressing over your salad. Serve and enjoy!

Nutritional Information:

- Calories: 441
- Total Fat: 16g
- Carbs: 71g
- Fiber: 13g
- Protein: 9g
- Sugar: 7g

10. Chicken Lunch Taco

Your child will surely enjoy this yummy healthy chicken taco recipe. Chicken is an excellent source of B vitamins which are helpful in preventing cataracts, skin disorders, helping to improve the nervous system, and boosting the immune system.

Preparation Time: 5 minutes

Total Cook Time: 20 minutes

Servings: 4

Ingredients:

- 1 chicken breast, boneless, skinless, cut into thin slices
- 2 medium oranges
- 1 cup cherry tomatoes
- 8 jumbo canned black olives
- 1 bell pepper, red, diced
- 2 cups iceberg lettuce, shredded
- 4-ounces cheddar cheese, shredded
- 4-ounces tortilla chips
- 2 teaspoons taco seasoning
- 4 soft tacos

Directions:

1. Heat your large skillet over medium heat, spray it with non-stick cooking spray. Add the chicken slices into skillet. You should cook your chicken for about 20 minutes or until cooked entirely through. Once cooked add the taco seasoning in with chicken and stir, then remove from heat.
2. Divide the seasoned chicken slices among four soft tacos. Add the remaining ingredients to tacos.
3. Serve chicken tacos and enjoy!

Nutritional Information:

- Calories: 344
- Total Fat: 14g
- Carbs: 33g
- Fiber: 5g
- Protein: 21g
- Sugar: 10g

11. Baked Vegetable Spring Rolls

This recipe for Spring rolls is packed with nutrients and great flavor. These are sure to be a favorite food in your child's lunch box. You might also want to add chicken or pork to this recipe for a different kind of Spring roll.

Preparation Time: 5 minutes

Total Cook Time: 14 minutes

Servings: 7

Ingredients:

- 1 tablespoon five spice blend (Chinese)
- 1 tablespoon soy sauce, low-sodium
- 1 cup Napa cabbage, shredded
- 1 cup bean sprouts
- 1 medium onion, diced
- 1 medium carrot, shredded
- 1 medium yellow bell pepper, diced
- 1 medium red bell pepper, diced
- 2 garlic cloves, crushed
- 0.5 tablespoons sesame oil
- 7 sheets phyllo dough

Directions:

1. Cut your phyllo pastry sheets in half so that you have 14 square sheets.

2. Preheat your oven to 390° Fahrenheit.

3. Cut your vegetables into thin strips, then heat some sesame oil in your wok over medium heat on the stovetop.

4. Add garlic into a wok and cook for 2 minutes.

5. Add the soy sauce, spice blend, cabbage, bean sprouts, onion, carrots, bell pepper slices.

6. Stir fry this mixture for about 4 minutes. Once done frying add to a colander and allow the juices to drain out and cool.

7. Take the phyllo sheet and place on top of another sheet in a diamond shape.

8. Add the vegetable filling just below the phyllo sheet's center, then wrap pastry to from the bottom up over the vegetable filling. Completely cover your filling.

9. Tuck the sides of the pastry to its center then roll it up. Repeat this process with the remaining ingredients until you have seven spring rolls completed.

10. Take a lined baking sheet and place your rolls onto it, then brush rolls with sesame oil on their tops. Bake for 12 minutes. Make sure to turn the rolls once during bake time.
11. Serve the Spring rolls when they are hot along with a dipping sauce of your choice and enjoy!

Nutritional Information:

- Calories: 99
- Total Fat: 2g
- Carbs: 16g
- Fiber: 1g
- Protein: 3g
- Sugar: 1g

12. Chopped Kale Salad

This kale salad is a perfect salad for kids. It offers a healthy recipe that contains cucumber which helps in weight loss, lowering blood sugar levels, balanced hydration, and digestive regularity due to the minerals and vitamins that it provides.

Preparation Time: 10 minutes

Servings: 6

Ingredients:

- 2 cups kale, chopped
- 1 teaspoon garlic powder
- 1 teaspoon lemon juice
- 1.5 teaspoons olive oil
- 0.25 cup red onion, chopped
- 1 avocado, cubed
- 1 cup mozzarella cheese, grated
- 1 cup cucumber, diced
- 1 cup cherry tomatoes, diced

Directions:

1. Add your vegetables and cheese to your salad bowl.
2. Add the garlic powder, olive oil, and lemon juice.
3. Mix salad to combine well. Serve and enjoy!

Nutritional Information:

- Calories: 155
- Total Fat: 14g
- Carbs: 9g
- Fiber: 3g
- Protein: 10g
- Sugar: 1g

13. Chicken Teriyaki Quesadilla

This recipe is a classic meal that can be enjoyed by the whole family as a main dish. The chicken in this recipe provides proteins and to make it more tasty for the kids to enjoy this healthy recipe!

Preparation Time: 5 minutes

Total Cook Time: 25 minutes

Servings: 4

Ingredients:

- 20-ounces cheddar cheese, grated
- 4 whole wheat tortillas
- 2 chicken breasts, skinless,
- boneless, cut into thin strips
- 2 cups broccoli florets
- 2 tablespoons cornstarch
- 2 tablespoons brown sugar
- 2 tablespoons water
- 1 tablespoon sesame oil
- 0.25 cup soy sauce, gluten-free
- 1 garlic clove, minced

Directions:

1. Whisk together soy sauce, garlic, sesame oil, brown sugar, and cornstarch, then set aside.
2. In a pot of boiling water add the broccoli, and boil for 5 minutes. Add ice cold water to stop the broccoli from cooking anymore then set aside.
3. Coat your skillet with non-stick cooking spray, add in some sesame oil over medium heat on the stovetop.

4. Cook the chicken strips in skillet for about 15 minutes or until the chicken is golden brown on all sides.

5. Place the broccoli in a colander to drain water. Add the broccoli into a skillet with cooked chicken, then stir in the garlic mixture. If you want to make the mix have a thinner consistency add a bit of water, then remove from heat.

6. Using another non-stick pan place it over medium heat. Place a tortilla into the pan, then add some of the chicken mixtures on top of tortilla on half of it. Sprinkle top of tortilla with cheese.

7. Cook tortilla for about 5 minutes or until the cheese has melted. Repeat this process with the remaining ingredients.

8. Serve these yummy quesadillas immediately and enjoy!

Nutritional Information:

- Calories: 351
- Total Fat: 12g
- Carbs: 92g
- Fiber: 2g
- Sugar: 6g

14. Chicken Pesto Kebabs

This healthy recipe will only take a few minutes to prepare. It will provide your child with a nutritious lunch that is full of protein.

Preparation Time: 10 minutes

Total Cook Time: 15 minutes

Servings: 6

Ingredients:

- 6 chicken breasts, skinless, boneless, cut into bite-size pieces
- 1.5 cup white mushrooms, sliced
- 2 teaspoon olive oil
- 2 red bell pepper, chopped to bite-size pieces
- 3 cups tortellini pasta, cooked and drained
- 0.5 cup pesto
- 15 skewers, wooden

Directions:

1. Add the cooked tortellini pasta into a pan. Add the pesto sauce, gently stirring to combine.
2. Add the mushroom, bell pepper, and olive oil into a skillet and sauté the vegetables until they are tender over medium heat.
3. Add the tortellini and pesto to the skillet and stir to combine, then remove skillet from heat.
4. Allow cooling enough so that you can add the pieces to the skewers, adding the chicken, veggies, and tortellini in any order.
5. Serve this dish warm or cold.

Nutritional Information:

- Calories: 390
- Total Fat: 21g
- Carbs: 32g
- Fiber: 1g
- Protein: 16g
- Sugar: 2g

15. Sweet Potato Quesadillas

If your child is bored with sandwiches, then why not try this sweet potato quesadillas recipe that is healthy and quick to prepare for at home or school.

Preparation Time: 10 minutes

Total Cook Time: 25 minutes

Servings: 4

Ingredients:

- 1 medium sweet potato
- 1 cup spinach, roughly chopped
- 2-ounces cheddar cheese, grated
- 8 medium tortillas
- 1 tablespoon taco seasoning
- 0.25 cup cilantro
- 15-ounces black beans, canned, drained and rinsed
- Serve with:
- 2 medium apples

Directions:

1. Poke holes into the sweet potato a few times by using a fork, then place in the microwave for 5 minutes. Allow potato to cool.

2. Cut open potato and scoop out the inner flesh and place in a bowl and mash.

3. Add black beans in with potato once they are rinsed and drained, also add the taco seasoning, and cilantro and mix to combine.

4. Heat a non-stick cooking skillet and add a tortilla. Spread some of the potato mixtures on it and top with some grated cheddar cheese and spinach, then top with another tortilla.

5. Over medium heat cook for four minutes, then flip and cook the other side or until the tortilla turns brown in color and the cheese has melted. Remove from skillet and slice quesadilla into quarters.

6. Repeat the process with the remaining ingredients.

7. Serve quesadillas warm with apple slices on the side and enjoy!

Nutritional Information:

- Calories: 552
- Total Fat: 12g
- Carbs: 92g
- Fiber: 14g
- Protein: 19g
- Sugar: 11g

16. Veggie Nuggets

This recipe is easy to prepare and healthy for kids as well as tasty.   The potatoes in the recipe containing essential nutrients that help the memory, learning, muscle movements, and even in the mood.

Preparation Time: 5 minutes

Total Cook Time: 40 minutes

Servings: 5

Ingredients:

- 0.75 cup plain breadcrumbs
- 1 lemon
- 0.25 teaspoon ground black pepper
- 0.5 cup frozen green peas
- 2.5 teaspoon olive oil
- 2 garlic cloves, minced
- 3 grated carrots medium
- 2 Russet potatoes, shredded
- 1 onion, diced

Directions:

1. In a skillet over medium heat on stovetop, add oil to warm, and add in the onion. Cook the onion for about 2 minutes.
2. Stir in the carrots, along with the potatoes and cook for an additional 5 minutes while stirring to combine.
3. Add the garlic, pepper, salt, and peas and cook for another 3 minutes.
4. Remove the skillet from heat and stir into the skillet add 0.25 cup breadcrumbs and lemon juice. Set aside to cool.
5. Prepare about 20 balls from the veggie mixture and place in the fridge for 30 minutes. Save remaining breadcrumbs in a dish.
6. Roll the veggie balls in the breadcrumbs until they are well coated.
7. In a medium skillet heat the extra oil, adding about 5 veggie balls at a time, cooking balls for 3 minutes or until they are browned. Place the cooked veggie balls on a paper towel to drain them.
8. Repeat the process with remaining veggie balls.
9. Serve and enjoy!

Nutritional Information:

- Calories: 232
- Total Fat: 7g
- Carbs: 36g
- Fiber: 4g
- Protein: 5g
- Sugar: 5g

Chapter 3. Healthy Children's Dinner Recipe Collection

17. Tender Crispy Baked Chicken

This is a great dinner recipe especially for children that have a problem digesting dairy. It has a high level of protein, chicken is also noticed as being useful in weight loss.

Preparation Time: 5 minutes

Total Cook Time: 30 minutes

Servings: 4

Ingredients:

- 1.5 teaspoon garlic powder
- sea salt to taste
- 1.5 teaspoon onion powder
- 1 teaspoon ground black pepper
- 3 teaspoons nutritional yeast
- 1.5 cup panko (Japanese breadcrumbs)
- 2 chicken breasts, skinless, boneless, sliced into thin strips
- 1 teaspoon lemon juice
- 1 cup plain rice milk

Directions:

1. Whisk the lemon juice and rice milk in a small dish.

2. Cut the chicken breasts into thin strips, then place pieces into milk mixture and place in the fridge for an hour.

3. Preheat your oven to 400° Fahrenheit, then line 2 baking sheets with foil.

4. Add the garlic powder, yeast, breadcrumbs, onion powder, pepper and salt into food processor and process until it is well broken down. Transfer mixture to a ziplock bag.

5. Add chicken strips into zip lock bag with batter and shake to evenly coat chicken pieces. Place chicken strips on baking sheets.

6. Bake your chicken for approximately 30 minutes or until it is fully cooked.

7. Serve and enjoy!

Nutritional Information:

- Calories: 244
- Total Fat: 7g
- Carb: 15g
- Fiber: 1g
- Protein: 24g
- Sugar: 4g

18. Butternut Squash Alfredo with Broccoli

This squash recipe is delicious and is sure to be a big win with the kids. It is a healthy and hearty dish that is nice for kids.

Preparation Time: 10 minutes

Total Cook Time: 30 minutes

Servings: 8

Ingredients:

- 1 cup butternut squash, sliced into 1-inch cubes
- 12-ounces pasta shapes
- 0.5 cup Parmesan cheese, shredded
- 0.25 tablespoons nutmeg
- 2 cups milk
- 3 tablespoons all-purpose flour
- 0.25 cup butter, unsalted
- 2 garlic cloves, minced
- 1 tablespoon olive oil
- 3 cups broccoli florets

Directions:

1. Preheat your oven to 400° Fahrenheit.

2. Add the butternut squash cubes and broccoli to a baking sheet. Drizzle with olive oil, salt, and pepper. Bake for 20 minutes.

3. Follow the package instructions when cooking pasta, then drain water out.

4. Add the garlic and butter to a small skillet over medium heat and allow butter to melt before adding the flour to pan. Whisk until smooth.

5. Cook for 2 minutes or so, then slowly add the milk and let the mixture boil while stirring occasionally. Add the nutmeg and cheese and mix until smooth.

6. Add the squash along with milk mixture into a blender and process until smooth.

7. Slowly add mixture over the pasta and stir to coat. Add the broccoli and enjoy!

Nutritional Information:

- Calories: 311
- Total Fat: 11g
- Carbs: 41g
- Fiber: 2g
- Protein: 10g
- Sugar: 5g

19. Crockpot Cheesy Vegetable Soup

This is a tasty, healthy recipe that will have your child eating vegetables. Vegetables provide us with lots of fiber which helps to reduce the risk of heart diseases, obesity, and type 2 diabetes.

Preparation Time: 5 minutes

Total Cook Time: 26 minutes

Servings: 10-12

Ingredients:

- 2 cups cheddar cheese, shredded
- 2 cups milk
- 1 teaspoon black pepper, ground
- 3 teaspoons mustard
- 0.5 cup all-purpose flour
- 4 teaspoons butter, unsalted
- 6 cups chicken broth, low-sodium
- 1 onion, chopped
- 2 cups broccoli florets
- 4 stalks celery, chopped
- 5 Russet potatoes, chopped
- 4 carrots, chopped

Directions:

1. Chop all of your vegetables: celery, carrots, potatoes, onion, and broccoli.
2. Add the chicken broth and chopped vegetables to your slow cooker. Cook for 6 hours on low or until the vegetables soften.
3. Prepare your sauce 30 minutes before serving. Add butter to a non-stick pan over medium heat on the stovetop, add flour, mustard, and salt. Stir to combine.
4. Add milk slowly to a pan and stir until mixture thickens.
5. Add the sauce into the slow cooker along with the cheese and stir to combine.
6. Serve and enjoy!

Nutritional Information:

- Calories: 315
- Fat: 14g
- Carbs: 33g
- Fiber: 3g
- Protein: 14g
- Sugar: 5g

20. Sweet and Sour Baked Cauliflower

This baked cauliflower recipe is full of flavor and nutritious for kids. It is a great dish to include with other healthy recipes. The deliciously sweet and sour sauce makes it irresistible to kids.

Preparation Time: 10 minutes

Total Cook Time: 45 minutes

Servings: 4

Ingredients:

- 3 tablespoons avocado oil
- 4 cups cauliflower, cut into bite-size pieces
- 1 cup rice, long grain

Sauce:

- 1 tablespoon cornstarch
- 2 tablespoons water
- 0.25 cup ketchup
- 0.25 tablespoon salt
- 0.5 tablespoons onion powder
- 1 tablespoon garlic powder
- 2 tablespoons soy sauce, gluten-free
- 0.33 cup vinegar cider
- 0.5 cup sugar
- Serve with:
- 1 stalk green onion, sliced
- 1 tablespoon sesame seeds

Directions:

1. Follow package directions for cooking rice, then set aside.

2. Preheat your oven to 425° Fahrenheit. Line a baking sheet with parchment paper.

3. Add cauliflower florets and avocado oil to a ziplock bag and shake to coat.

4. Spread the cauliflower florets across the baking sheet and bake until lightly browned.

5. Set oven to broil and cook for 4 minutes on this setting.

6. In a saucepan add all the sauce ingredients to pan except for water and cornstarch.

7. In a mixing bowl, whisk the water and cornstarch together, after cornstarch is fully dissolved add mix to sauce mixture. Stir to combine and cook until sauce becomes thick.

8. Add your roasted cauliflower to the sauce and toss to coat.

9. Serve with rice topped with onions, and sesame seeds and enjoy!

Nutritional Information:

- Calories: 440
- Fat: 12g
- Carbs: 76g
- Fiber: 3g
- Protein: 7g
- Sugar: 30g

21. Vegetarian Black Bean Tortillas

An easy and quick meal to prepare. It is a healthy meal that includes black beans which are a rich source of protein and fiber; both of which are essential components for kid's healthy growth.

Preparation Time: 10 minutes

Total Cook Time: 25 minutes

Servings: 10

Ingredients:

- 2 cups black beans
- 12 whole wheat tortillas
- 4-ounces Monterrey Jack cheese, shredded
- 0.75 cup frozen corn
- 1 red bell pepper, diced
- 10-ounces frozen spinach, thawed and drained
- 0.25 cup lime juice
- 2-ounces cream cheese, low-fat
- 0.25 teaspoon ground black pepper
- 0.5 teaspoon salt
- 0.5 teaspoon ground cumin
- 1 garlic clove
- 2 teaspoons salsa

Directions:

1. Preheat an oven to 425° Fahrenheit.
2. Put 0.75 cup beans in a blender. Add garlic, salsa, lime juice, cream cheese, pepper, salt and blend until smooth.
3. Next, transfer your mixture to a mixing bowl then add grated cheese, spinach, corn, bell pepper, and rest of the beans and combine thoroughly.
4. Place 0.5 cup mixture on every tortilla and roll up tightly.
5. Place the rolled tortillas on an oiled baking sheet.
6. Place the baking sheet with tortillas into the oven and bake for 25 minutes or until golden brown and become crisp.
7. Serve warm and enjoy!

Nutritional Information:

- Calories: 314
- Total Fat: 8g
- Carbs: 46g
- Fiber: 6g
- Protein: 13g
- Sugar: 1g

22. Baked Pumpkin Macaroni & Cheese

This recipe is one of the best-baked macaroni dishes. It is a healthy meal that is packed with nutrients. Serve this dish with some fresh fruits and veggies to make it a kid-friendly dinner.

Preparation Time: 5 minutes

Total Cook Time: 40 minutes

Servings: 6

Ingredients:

- 8-ounces macaroni pasta (dry)
- 0.25 tablespoons black pepper, ground
- 0.25 tablespoons salt
- 0.25 tablespoons garlic powder
- 0.25 tablespoons sage, ground
- 0.5 tablespoons onion powder
- 1 tablespoon mustard, ground
- 2 tablespoons all-purpose flour
- 2-ounces Parmesan cheese
- 8-ounces cheddar cheese
- 0.5 cup Greek yogurt, plain
- 1 cup pumpkin, pureed canned
- 1 cup milk

Directions:

1. Preheat your oven to 350° Fahrenheit. Grease a medium baking dish and set it aside.
2. Cook the noodles for five minutes, drain them without rinsing.
3. Add the yogurt, milk, pumpkin into the greased baking dish.
4. Add the seasonings, cheddar, and Parmesan cheese, flour into a mixing bowl and toss to combine.
5. Add this mixture to the baking dish followed by the noodles. Combine mix by stirring gently.
6. Bake mixture for 35 minutes then serve and enjoy!

Nutritional Information:

- Carbs: 387
- Total Fat: 18g
- Fiber: 2g
- Protein: 20g
- Sugar: 4g

23. Cauliflower Pizza Crust

This is excellent comfort food for kids. The cauliflower offers antioxidants which will help protect body cells from inflammation and from dangerous free radicals. It is not only a healthy recipe but a tasty one too!

Preparation Time: 10 minutes

Total Cook Time: 30 minutes

Servings: 4

Ingredients:

- 1 egg
- 0.5 teaspoons ground black pepper
- 0.5 teaspoon salt
- 0.5 teaspoon dried oregano
- 0.5 dried parsley
- 0.5 teaspoon dried basil
- 10-ounces Parmesan cheese, grated
- 30-ounces Mozzarella cheese, grated
- 1 cauliflower, chopped into florets

Toppings:

- 1 cup pizza sauce
- 0.5 cup sliced white mushrooms
- 1 cup green bell pepper, diced
- 8 jumbo black olives, sliced

Directions:

1. Preheat your oven to 400° Fahrenheit, then grease a pan.
2. In your blender pulse the cauliflower florets until crumbly. Transfer to a microwave bowl and cook for 3 minutes in a microwave until tender.

3. Allow mixture to cool then wring florets to remove extra moisture in a clean piece of cheesecloth. Transfer the cauliflower to a mixing bowl.

4. Add the Parmesan, 0.25 cup Mozzarella, basil, parsley, oregano, salt, and pepper into mixing bowl and stir to combine.

5. Add in the egg and stir to combine.

6. Place the dough into pan and shape into a crust. Set aside.

7. Bake the crust in your oven until crust is golden brown for about 20 minutes.

8. Evenly spread your pizza sauce on the crust and add the remaining toppings and cheese on top.

9. Put your pizza back into the oven and back for an additional 10 minutes.

10. Allow cooling then serve and enjoy!

Nutritional Information:

- Calories: 167
- Total Fat: 7g
- Carbs: 13g
- Fiber: 5g
- Protein: 13g
- Sugar: 5g

24. Spaghetti Squash Bake

This dish is a mild-flavored recipe that is rich in carbohydrates and is nutritious, and it should be on your list of healthy recipes for your kids.

Preparation Time: 10 minutes

Total Cook Time: 38 minutes

Servings: 8

Ingredients:

- 2 medium spaghetti squash
- 0.25 cup all-purpose flour
- 0.125 cup Parmesan cheese, grated
- 2 cups cheddar cheese, grated
- 0.125 tablespoons black pepper, ground
- 0.125 salt
- 1 cup vegetable broth
- 1.5 cup milk
- 3 cups broccoli florets, chopped
- 2 cloves garlic, minced
- 1 tablespoon olive oil

Directions:

1. Preheat your oven to 375° Fahrenheit.
2. Cook your squash in a crock-pot, then use a fork and scoop its strands. Add the strands into a baking dish.
3. Place a skillet over medium heat and cook olive oil. Add the chopped onions and garlic and allow to cook for about 4 minutes.
4. Add the broccoli and let cook until it is a little chewy and firm.

5. Add the flour and reduce heat to simmer, cooking for another 4 minutes.

6. Add the milk and vegetable broth to small saucepan. Whisk and increase the heat until it boils and becomes nice and smooth.

7. Season with salt and pepper, once it thickens remove from heat. Add cheddar cheese to mix and stir until it melts.

8. Add the onions, garlic, and broccoli to the baking dish along with spaghetti squash. Add the milk batter over the spaghetti squash in baking dish and top with Parmesan cheese.

9. Bake your squash bake for 30 minutes or until golden brown, then serve and enjoy!

Nutritional Information:

- Calories: 222
- Total Fat: 13g
- Carbs: 15g
- Fiber: 2g
- Protein: 11g
- Sugar: 6g

Chapter 4. Healthy Children's Snack Recipe Collection

25. Cucumber Cups

This healthy recipe is refreshing and will help keep your child full until the next meal. It is an excellent snack that is rich in water making it an excellent hydrating food source.

Preparation Time: 5 minutes

Total Cook Time: 5 minutes

Servings: 4

Ingredients:

- 4 eggs, boiled
- 1 carrot, medium, peeled and cut
- 1.08 teaspoon paprika
- 1.08 teaspoon ground black pepper
- 1 teaspoon mustard
- 0.25 cup light mayonnaise
- 2 cucumbers

Directions:

1. Add the eggs into a pot of boiling water and boil for 5 minutes. Allow the eggs to cool for about 10 minutes after boiling them. Clean and peel the eggs in some cold water.
2. Cut the cucumbers into 1.5-inch pieces eliminating the ends so it can sit on a level surface.
3. Scoop out the cucumber center using a spoon.
4. Combine the eggs mayonnaise, mustard, paprika, salt, and pepper, and fill cucumber cups with mixture.
5. Serve carrots with cucumber cups and enjoy!

Nutritional Information:

- Calories: 133
- Total Fat: 7g
- Carbs: 9g
- Fiber: 1g
- Protein: 7g
- Sugar: 4g

26. Frozen Yogurt Pops

When it comes to preparing frozen yogurt popsicles at home, the sky is the limit!   Allow your child to choose a fruit that he or she loves when preparing pops. This is a healthy recipe for kids that they will surely enjoy indulging in!

Preparation Time: 4 hours and 30 minutes

Servings: 4

Ingredients:

- 1 cup plain yogurt
- 0.125 cup honey
- 1 cup mixed berries, frozen
- 1 medium banana

Directions:

1. In your blender add all your ingredients, then process until smooth.
2. Add to paper cups then cover with a bit of foil. Using the popsicle stick pierce the middle of the foil. The foil will help to keep the stick in place.
3. Freeze until solid and enjoy!

Nutritional Information:

- Calories: 114
- Total Fat: 1g
- Carbs: 24g
- Fiber: 2g
- Protein: 3g
- Sugar: 16g

27. Pumpkin Hummus

This is a great healthy pumpkin hummus recipe for kids. It is easy and straightforward to prepare. The pumpkin is rich in carotenoid compounds that function as antioxidants which help protect the body against certain cancers.

Preparation Time: 5 minutes

Servings: 3 cups

Ingredients:

- 2 cans chickpeas, drained
- 0.25 teaspoons paprika
- 0.25 cup olive oil
- 1 teaspoon ground cumin
- 1.5 teaspoons lemon juice
- 1 teaspoon salt
- 2 garlic cloves, minced
- 2 teaspoons tahini
- 15-ounces canned pumpkin puree

Directions:

1. Mix all of your ingredients in your blender, and process until smooth. If too thick add olive oil.
2. Serve with vegetables and crackers and enjoy!

Nutritional Information:

- Calories: 504
- Total Fat: 28g
- Carbs: 52g
- Fiber: 17g
- Protein: 15g
- Sugar: 4g

28. Carrot Chips

Carrot chips are an easy snack to prepare for your kids that is healthy. This is a different way to include veggies in the diet of kids that are picky eaters.

Preparation Time: 5 minutes

Total Cook Time: 20 minutes

Servings: 4

Ingredients:

- 0.125 tablespoon salt
- 1 tablespoon olive oil
- 4 medium carrots, peeled

Directions:

1. Preheat your oven to 350° Fahrenheit.
2. Slice the carrots into strips, using a vegetable peeler.
3. Use oil to grease pan, and place single layer of carrot strips on it.
4. Toss to coat carrot strips with olive oil.
5. Sprinkle with salt to taste
6. Bake carrots until crispy and enjoy!

Nutritional Information:

- Calories: 54
- Total Fat: 3g
- Carbs: 5g
- Fiber: 1g
- Protein: 0g
- Sugar: 2g

29. No-Bake Carrot Cake Bites

This is a healthy snack that requires no cooking. Carrots are a great source of vitamin A which helps to improve eyesight and reduces night blindness.

Preparation Time: 20 minutes

Servings: 16 bites

Ingredients:

- 3 carrots, medium
- 1.08 teaspoon sea salt
- 0.5 teaspoons ground ginger
- 0.5 teaspoons nutmeg
- 1 teaspoon cinnamon
- 1 cup dry oats
- 1 teaspoon almond butter
- 0.5 cup chopped pecans
- 6 Medjool dates

Directions:

1. Process your carrots in your food processor until they are finely ground then transfer to a mixing bowl.
2. Place the pecans and dates into food processor and process until well combined.
3. Return the carrots to process then add the rest of the ingredients.
4. Process until a dough forms, then roll into balls.
5. Roll the dough balls and store them in a sealed container.
6. You can refrigerate this snack for a week.

Nutritional Information:

- Calories: 81
- Total Fat: 3g
- Carbs: 12g
- Fiber: 2g
- Protein: 1g

30. Sweet Spinach Muffins

These spinach muffins are a delicious snack that is certain to become a favorite of your kids.

Preparation Time: 10 minutes

Total Cook Time: 28 minutes

Servings: 18 muffins

Ingredients:

- 1 tablespoon vanilla extract
- 1 large egg
- 0.5 cup butter, unsalted
- 6-ounces spinach, frozen, thawed, drained
- 1 large banana
- 0.5 cup honey
- 0.75 cup milk
- 0.25 tablespoon salt
- 0.5 tablespoon baking soda
- 2 tablespoons baking powder
- 1.5 tablespoons cinnamon powder
- 2 cups whole wheat flour
- 18 cupcake liners, standard

Directions:

1. Preheat your oven to 350° Fahrenheit.
2. Spray cooking spray in muffin silicone cups then line them in the muffin pan.
3. In a mixing bowl, mix your ingredients.
4. Melt the butter then blend all the wet ingredients in a blender until smooth.
5. Add the wet ingredients in with your dry ingredients, stir to combine.
6. Spoon mixture into muffin cups and bake for 28 minutes or until muffins are firm.
7. Cool muffins, serve and enjoy!

Nutritional Information:

- Calories: 140
- Total Fat: 11g
- Carbs: 20g
- Fiber: 2g
- Protein: 2g
- Sugar: 9g

Conclusion

I hope that you will use this collection of healthy kids recipes to help create a healthy daily diet for your child. Take some time to really discover the healthy foods that your child likes and try to integrate them into your family meals. I am sure you will be preparing healthy recipes for your child that will make them have a positive outlook towards healthy eating. Please feel free to adjust or tweak this collection of recipes to suit the personal tastes of your child, so hopefully, it will make feeding time not only healthy but more fun for your child. Perhaps you too will also enjoy these healthy recipes—these are foods that you can enjoy with your child while you are strengthening your bonds. Why not spend some quality time with your child while you share some healthy and tasty dishes!

About the Author

Born in New Germantown, Pennsylvania, Stephanie Sharp received a Masters degree from Penn State in English Literature. Driven by her passion to create culinary masterpieces, she applied and was accepted to The International Culinary School of the Art Institute where she excelled in French cuisine. She has married her cooking skills with an aptitude for business by opening her own small cooking school where she teaches students of all ages.

Stephanie's talents extend to being an author as well and she has written over 400 e-books on the art of cooking and baking that include her most popular recipes.

Sharp has been fortunate enough to raise a family near her hometown in Pennsylvania where she, her husband and children live in a beautiful rustic house on an extensive piece of land. Her other passion is taking care of the furry members of her family which include 3 cats, 2 dogs and a potbelly pig named Wilbur.

Watch for more amazing books by Stephanie Sharp coming out in the next few months.

Author's Afterthoughts

I am truly grateful to you for taking the time to read my book. I cherish all of my readers! Thanks ever so much to each of my cherished readers for investing the time to read this book!

With so many options available to you, your choice to buy my book is an honour, so my heartfelt thanks at reading it from beginning to end!

I value your feedback, so please take a moment to submit an honest and open review on Amazon so I can get valuable insight into my readers' opinions and others can benefit from your experience.

Thank you for taking the time to review!

Stephanie Sharp

For announcements about new releases, please

follow my author page on Amazon.com!

(Look for the Follow Bottom under the photo)

You can find that at:

https://www.amazon.com/author/stephanie-sharp

*or Scan **QR-code** below.*

Made in the USA
Monee, IL
29 June 2022

98828492R00069